TWO EQUALS ONE

WORKBOOK

TWO EQUALS ONE WORKBOOK

JIMMY ROLLINS & IRENE ROLLINS

W Publishing Group
An Imprint of Thomas Nelson

Two Equals One Workbook

Published in Nashville, Tennessee, by W Publishing, an imprint of Thomas Nelson.

Published in association with The Bindery Agency, www.thebinderyagency.com.
Contributing Editor: Heather Preston

ISBN 978-1-4003-4756-8 (ePub)
ISBN 978-1-4003-4755-1 (softcover)

Printed in the United States of America

24 25 26 27 28 LBC 6 5 4 3 2

CONTENTS

INTRODUCTION

GET READY

Are you ready to get healthy in your marriage? Are you tired of arguing more than agreeing—of feeling more tension than chemistry in your marriage? Tired of having more stress than sex? Are you ready to find solutions to the struggles?

It's time to step into a new season of love, laughter, and longevity!

We didn't write this book to just help people survive in marriage—we wrote it to show others how to thrive! You don't have to be miserable in marriage, and the goal isn't just to "make it" the longest. The goal is to discover your united identity—the power of two equals one.

Through our own personal stories, as well as accounts of couples we've coached, we want to walk you through what it means to do the work of marriage. We want to provide you with the tools that have helped so many reach their thriving potential in marriage—including us! Each challenge is designed to be a resource—something that you can actually use long after you're done with this workbook. We use each one of these exercises to this day—many of them we've modified or personalized to suit our needs, which is something we recommend each of you do as well!

As you go through the exercises, the goal isn't ever to get the "right" answer, but rather to learn more about your spouse and yourself so that you're better able to understand each other's needs. Each exercise corresponds to the chapter in the book *Two Equals One* with the same number.

We want to challenge you as we walk through these next eighteen exercises to do like the psalmist encourages—to be "slow to get angry" (Psalm 145:8 NLT).

Easier said than done, right? We get that. But the reason we are so adamant about this is because we've experienced the damage of words flung in anger.

Sometimes it's important to take a breath.

Pause, and revisit the subject when you're in a better headspace.

We're so proud of you for doing the work of marriage, and we understand the urgency you may be feeling, but it's important that you do not rush through these challenges. Sometimes it's tough to be present when you're feeling a certain way toward your spouse. Maybe there's built-up resentment or frustration, unforgiveness or secrets between you. Whatever you're feeling, don't ignore it. Don't rush past it. Let this workbook be like your personal trainer.

In order to turn your struggle into strength, you have to lean in. If you've ever spent much time in the gym, you've undoubtedly heard the expression "a good burn." What they're saying is that they can feel the muscles burning, which means that the exercise is making them stronger. Our instinct is to avoid the burn—really any kind of discomfort. But just like at the gym, in marriage if you want to see results, if you want health and longevity, you have to lean into the burn. You have to acknowledge the discomfort, the emotions, and the tension.

The good news? It makes you stronger! This practice will lead to health, and you will begin to see growth in your ability to communicate and meet each other's needs. We truly believe that as you apply these biblical principles to your marriage, you will see the same transformative power we experienced in our marriage!

CHALLENGE ONE

PICTURE THIS

Review: Chapter 1 of *Two Equals One* (pages 3–11)

Have you ever heard the phrase "picture this"? It can get watered down to the point of sounding gimmicky, but there is a powerful scripture we often refer to when we're in a season where we feel like we can't find our way:

Where there is no vision, the people perish...

PROVERBS 29:18 KJV

In order for us to grow together, we need to share a vision. Now, we've heard this verse used to suggest that married couples do everything from inscribing their family motto on a sign for their home, to mapping out paralegal-style their future career and life goals. What we want you to do today is much simpler but, in our experience, far more lasting.

We struggled for years without a vision. We would often find ourselves strapped financially, arguing about the kids. I would want to move forward and she would be stuck, or I would be stuck and she would want to move. Maybe you're fighting because you have no goals. Or maybe it feels like you have opposing goals and you can't see how they'll ever come together.

Vision is simply getting a picture of your future purpose. It's always connected to what matters most to you, what drives you. That thing that is intrinsically part of your identity. Once you get a picture, you can press forward.

Not only can God redeem any situation, but he can restore and use the brokenness too. Nothing is wasted in his hands.

***TWO EQUALS ONE*, PAGE 8**

So . . . what does it look like?

Seasons change, but your vision remains steadfast. Once you have a picture of your future, you're not relying on what you're currently looking at to determine what you see. Vision doesn't go by what's in front of us to determine the goal. It's not limited by a situation or circumstance.

Today, we aren't making word art for your home or categorizing your life in a three-ring binder. Instead, we want you to mark this moment in your journey—specifically, your *relationship* journey. Ask yourself: *Where am I now and where do I want to be?*

Now step back for a moment.

Breathe.

First, take some time to reflect on your marriage. Consider each other and resist the urge to rush through as you ask the following four questions . . .

1. What is our vision for our **marriage**? What do we want to accomplish together? No matter what's behind us, what is ahead of us that we can reach for together?

2. What is our vision for **tension**? How are we going to act or respond during seasons of tension? Out of this you will discover your rules of engagement. When fights occur (and they will), what are your ground rules that ensure you don't cause each other unnecessary hurt or cause one another to shut down, making any communication unproductive? This particular vision helped us personally move from rupture to repair—it turned struggling into strength training and equipped us for future challenges. We'll focus more on this later, but think of these like the rules in any sport—they exist to prevent an athlete from being injured. In marriage, it's important to think like a team and to look out for one another.

3. What is our vision for **children**? How many? What are our educational goals for our children? What are our spiritual goals for our children?

Proverbs 22:6 tells us, "Train up a child in the way he should go; even when he is old he will not depart from it." Scripture literally teaches us to be guided by vision.

4. What is our vision for our **careers**? And more importantly, what are our nonnegotiables? You must have a vision for your career; however, you must also determine what your nonnegotiables are. Nonnegotiables are essential values that prioritize the things that are most important. Having a vision for your career is important, but not at the expense of maintaining your family as a priority. This is where you both need to list specific ways you want to guard your relationship and protect any potential children from taking second place.

Whatever you answered to these questions, there is no "right" or "wrong." However, we truly believe that by the end of this journey together, you will see a marked improvement in your relationship, and we would encourage you both to sign in the space below and write the date! This is how we create a picture worth referencing down the road. We strongly encourage reviewing your vision together at least once a month.

....
Signature

....
Date

NOTES

CHALLENGE TWO

MARRIAGE ER | EMOTIONAL RESPONSE

It's ironic, isn't it? The same recipe for romance can also wreak havoc.

***TWO EQUALS ONE*, PAGE 18**

Review: Chapter 2 of *Two Equals One* (pages 13–25)

We talked a lot in chapter 2 about differences. How differences naturally cause division.

Often when our differences start causing division, we avoid them—our instinct being to preserve peace even if it's not truly peace but rather a facade. Meanwhile, we wrestle internally with our feelings, and as they accumulate, they make it even more difficult to get to the source of our emotions.

We'll never forget the time we were working with a couple and the coaching session was like being in the emergency room. Have you ever been rushed to the ER? All you can think about is how much it hurts—you don't know why or how to fix it, you're just in pain. All you can focus on is how badly you hurt, and you're thinking *please make it stop hurting.*

Troy and Trisha's marriage was in the ER. They'd had a huge fight. All he expressed was anger and all she felt was fear. It's crazy how in these moments we forget about all the other emotions—we get stuck in the one we're feeling most in that moment.

We basically had Troy and Trisha come in the triage and assess their emotions as they would a medical condition. Troy's anger was like a symptom, masking untreated hurt and confusion. Trisha's fear was underlying uncertainty and shame. Once we sat down and dealt with the present pain, they were able to put definition to their emotions.

Emotions are intuitive indicators that let you know that it's time to heal the wound announced by the pain. It's time to multiply the productive emotions and find healing. In order to do this, we have to evaluate our own thoughts and feelings.

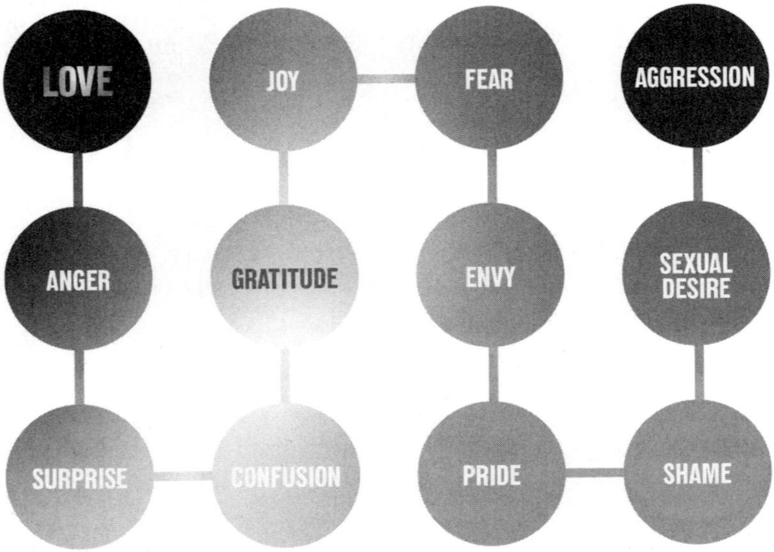

This is such an important step in moving forward in your relationship and making progress in your marriage!

The challenge for today is to answer the questions listed here and then to organize your feelings. The goal of the emotion word bank you see at the bottom of the previous page and the diagram here is to process and logically evaluate the differences that cause disruption in your relationship. Once you have answered each question, the diagram will give you a more concise visual of your internal feelings.

This will be an independent challenge because it is imperative that you are as honest as possible with each answer. Resist the temptation to answer these questions for your spouse—don't assume what the other is thinking or feeling.

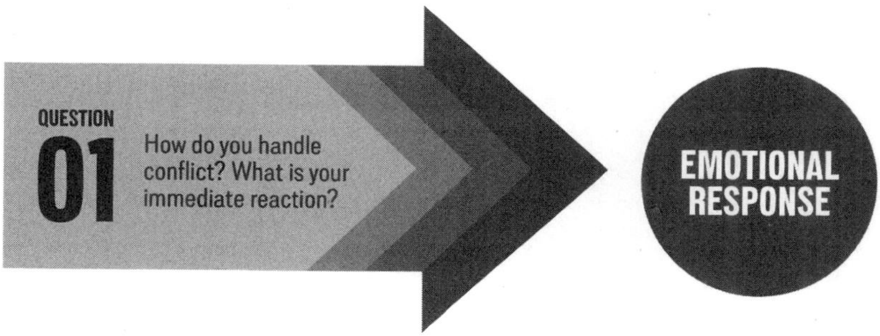

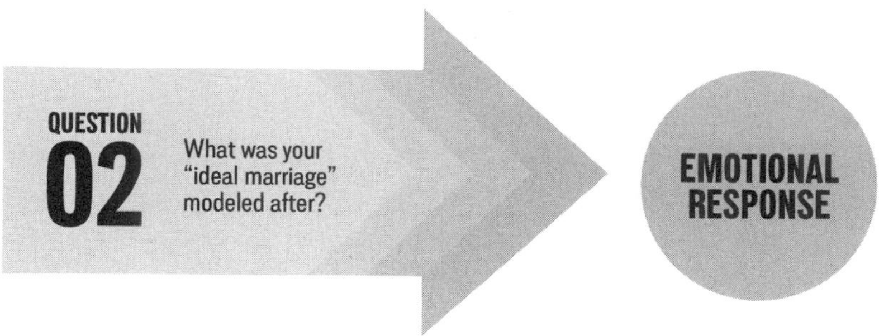

QUESTION 03 What is the argument that creates the most anxiety in your heart?

EMOTIONAL RESPONSE

The goal of analyzing your emotions is to discover why you are feeling the way you are feeling so that your emergency room situation can produce a healthy response.

I'll never forget my own literal emergency room situation. About ten years ago, I was suffering from severe stomach pain. I kept going back to the ER repeatedly until I was finally diagnosed with a gallbladder issue; the pain uncovered the actual problem. Don't dismiss the pain—it's actually productive. It has a purpose. Don't be frustrated because emotions don't fix the problem; they may not make the pain go away, but they uncover the main problem that you don't yet see.

CHALLENGE THREE

SICK AS YOUR SECRETS

Let all bitterness and wrath and anger and clamor [perpetual animosity, resentment, strife, fault-finding] and slander be put away from you, along with every kind of malice [all spitefulness, verbal abuse, malevolence].

EPHESIANS 4:31 AMP

Review: Chapter 3 of *Two Equals One* (pages 27–42)

Your marriage will always be as sick as your secrets. The good news is that honesty can bring healing, but before we can be honest with each other, we have to be honest with ourselves. This isn't always a "big" sin issue.

Remember the mosquito we mentioned in chapter 3? You often don't know you've been bitten until your body itches. In the same way, you may have let resentment build up toward your spouse without ever addressing the initial hurt.

Your secret may be a weakness that you don't want to admit—an area of vulnerability that you worry will make your spouse think less of you. Before we move ahead, take a long, hard look and examine yourself—your secrets, wants, and unspoken needs. Pray and be honest and vulnerable with God.

Is there something you've been keeping from your spouse? An addiction you've been covering up? A moment from your past that you've been too ashamed to talk about? Or maybe a dream that you've been keeping to yourself?

IRENE

Real talk begins with you. Before I went to rehab, our marriage was at its worst. Mostly out of desperation, we decided to get help. The first thing our counselor gave us was a questionnaire that we were instructed to fill out separately. It was a series of deeply personal questions that provided background for our potential reactions and responses so that the counselor could help us navigate. Without my knowing, Jimmy actually read mine. When he admitted this to me, I was outraged. It was a total violation of privacy!

But what I had written had utterly rocked him. You see, I had been honest in my answers and admitted many previous traumas I had experienced; from abuse to sexual assault, I had written things down that I had never spoken about. He was shocked that we had been married over a decade, and he didn't know any of it.

Just as the counselor needed insight to help us navigate marriage, my husband needed insight to understand me. As inappropriate as his methods may have been, reading my questionnaire had finally given him some definition to our dysfunction. He finally understood my affection-and-intimacy issues. It helped him contextualize my communication—or lack thereof.

This exercise is about being honest with yourself. You can't be honest with your spouse until you can be honest with yourself. If you want to create a safe place where you and your spouse can be transparent and vulnerable, you have to be willing to do the work on yourself first.

Once you are able to be honest with yourself, write a list of things you have been withholding that you want to share with your spouse. If you have a more serious confession, we recommend you talk to a marriage counselor first. Consider bringing a paid professional in to help guide the process and facilitate conversation.

Five areas of honesty:

1. Honesty about past trauma: What in your past was traumatic that you have never dealt with?
2. Honesty about family dysfunction: What family issues did you grow up with that feel shameful to talk about? Remember: what you protect you often project.
3. Honesty about financial secrets: Budgets are no one's favorite subject, but money can easily become a stumbling block in marriage. Transparency and accountability are the only way to eliminate this obstacle, but that requires honesty.
4. Honesty about past dysfunctional relationships: This isn't purely about previous romantic relationships but about understanding the relational dysfunction you've experienced so that you don't repeat those patterns in the future or project mistrust on your spouse as a result of previous trauma.
5. Honesty about sexual secrets: Are there past sexual secrets that prevent you from truly being present or fully intimate?

Many of these are things you will need to work out with a professional before you attempt to work out with your spouse. It's impossible for the love of God to heal what you continue to cover up. First John 4:18 tells us, "There is no fear in love, but perfect love casts out fear."

Whatever you need to confide in your spouse, remember that love is stronger than fear. But love invites, it never imposes. Love never forces its way, which means that if we don't allow our spouse in, if we continue to hide things and cover up, love can't heal. The only way to experience freedom in love is through honesty.

CHALLENGE FOUR

RECONCILABLE DIFFERENCES

The true version of two equals one is an invitation to love everything that is different about your spouse.

***TWO EQUALS ONE*, PAGES 44–45**

Review: Chapter 4 of *Two Equals One* (pages 43–52)

It's easy to view working on your marriage as an attempt to "fix" your spouse. But that's simply not what it's about. Working on your marriage starts with *you*. That being said, differences can feel impossible at times. The opposites that attracted initially can feel like opposition, and what we used to love in our spouse, we can grow to resent.

Ever been hungry while riding in the car and you're trying to decide what to eat? Of course he wants steak. Of course you want sushi. Of course you know the right way to go and he's positive he doesn't need directions!

Differences show up in many forms, but could you imagine being married to a carbon copy of yourself? Life would be unbearably boring. Here's the thing: differences become irreconcilable only when you refuse to accept that the goal is not to think alike but rather to think together.

In Psalm 133 (NLT), King David celebrates the beauty of living "in harmony." Now, David was a musician and harmony is a musical term. In a harmony, you have to be singing the same melody but different notes. It creates a powerful effect that's unattainable by an individual vocalist. But in the same way that harmony requires a shared melody, you and your spouse have to share a common vision in order for your differences to harmonize.

Differences don't have to divide; they can actually showcase our unique gifts in a way that's like a well-constructed harmony! God didn't design you to fail. Two can equal one, but you have to face what you fear and not try to "fix" it.

Individually, write a list of differences that you have rejected versus accepted.

For example: "My spouse needs space and doesn't want to talk right away when they're frustrated, whereas I want to address the issue immediately."

Then, write a "turnaround" statement. A turnaround statement is a way of reframing your differences so that rather than clashing, they harmonize. An example of a turnaround for the previous difference might be: "I'm going to give my spouse time to collect their thoughts before engaging."

If you can't think of any differences immediately, ask yourself:

What are the differences we have in parenting our kids?

Example: "My spouse is old school when it comes to discipline, but I prefer gentle parenting."

Turnaround example: "We both love and want to guide our children. Establishing boundaries works in tandem with communicating wants and needs."

What are the differences in our sexual appetites?

Example: "I want sex more often, but I don't want to initiate it because I want to feel pursued."

Turnaround: "I recognize that sometimes the signals I send might convey more annoyed than amorous, so I will adjust my mental script to think positively about my spouse's desire for me."

What are the differences in how we spend our time?

Example: "I feel most relaxed when there's an established agenda, but my spouse wants to unwind by not doing anything."

Turnaround: "I'm going to schedule time regularly to accommodate my spouse's need for unstructured relaxation."

NOTES

CHALLENGE FIVE

SLOW JAMS

Then the LORD God said, "It is not good for the man to be alone."

GENESIS 2:18 NLT

Review: Chapter 5 of *Two Equals One* (pages 53–63)

As we read in chapter 5, it's actually been scientifically proven: Loneliness kills. We weren't created to do life alone. And although this is true, you may be reading this and feeling alone in your marriage.

Sadly, this is because many of us (we experienced this ourselves!) have been fed society's version of love. Many of us got our ideas of love from movies or music. (Personally, I got mine from '80s/'90s/2000s R&B!). But the messages in these slow jams can jam up your ability to actually experience true love.

Many of us have internalized the messages, rehearsed how they are supposed to feel, what they are supposed to look like . . . and one day you wake up and realize your marriage isn't that. In order to experience real love—the kind that transforms your marriage and fills you with purpose and power—you have to have a proper understanding of love. It's the first step to freedom in your relationship.

Today's exercise is to independently evaluate your definition of love. We encourage you to list ways that your love has conditions, limitations, and restrictions. Ask yourself:

1. Where did I get my definition of love?
2. Was that model healthy or unhealthy?
3. If your love is conditional, it probably fails to have capacity.

If you're unsure whether or not your love is conditional, ask yourself if your definition of love includes empathy, compassion, or forgiveness.

Below are five essential truths the Bible gives us about love:

1. "Love never gives up.
2. Love cares more for others than for self.
3. Love doesn't want what it doesn't have . . .
4. [Love] always looks for the best,
5. [Love] never looks back, but keeps going to the end." (1 Corinthians 13:6–7 MSG)

These five truths define love. If you haven't had a good model, know this: It is impossible to give away something you've never received. If you've never experienced this kind of love, there's a prayer on page 60 of the *Two Equals One* for you.

Once, we coached a couple who were from dramatically different cultural backgrounds. Things they thought they were confident in navigating before marriage suddenly seemed insurmountable. Each thought the problem stemmed from the other person.

When they took a hard look at their personal definitions of love, they realized they each had conditions—they each had internalized resentment as a result of unmet needs that they hadn't given voice to. Once they recognized these needs, they were able to formulate a plan to move forward.

Conditions result in restrictions—if you have conditions, your own restrictions are holding you back.

What I couldn't see then was that loving Irene through the pain was actually allowing for a much greater work to be done. Our pain had a much greater purpose.

***TWO EQUALS ONE*, PAGE 62**

Honestly journal your responses to the three questions on the previous page and then evaluate whether your definition of *love* is more influenced by Scripture or by society. In what ways can you redefine *love* based on what you've been learning so far?

NOTES

CHALLENGE SIX

PRACTICE MAKES PERMANENT

"Ask, and it will be given to you . . ."
MATTHEW 7:7

Review: Chapter 6 of *Two Equals One* (pages 69–77)

In case you're wondering, no, today's challenge isn't about getting your spouse a material gift! Today is about making sure your spouse feels heard. In marriage, simply saying that you're "for" each other isn't enough. Sometimes we need to *show* our spouse.

These next few challenges, we're going to be talking about laughter. But laughter is in large part a result of good communication. Communication isn't always what you're saying, it's how you're caring. You can't genuinely laugh when you have a wall up or you're tense and guarded, but sometimes in order to help our spouse let down their guard, we need to demonstrate our love. We've all heard it said that actions speak louder than words, and today we're going to put this into practice; today's challenge is about showing how you care.

Write down a concern or request your spouse has made recently that you haven't followed up on. It doesn't have to be a major undertaking; it can be something as simple as doing the dishes! A small gesture that makes your spouse feel seen.

Maybe it's closing cabinet drawers or dropping off the dry cleaning—whatever it is, make a point of getting it done for your spouse.

If you can't think of anything, ask your spouse for a way that you can help them this week. Make sure that it's something specific. Practice doesn't make perfect, it makes permanent! Get out your calendar, your phone, or whatever is most accessible to you and schedule.

JIMMY

I remember our counselor assigning this same challenge to us. That week I happened to notice that Irene had made a note scheduling in a reminder to "hug Jimmy." This seemed absolutely ridiculous to me—*you need a reminder to hug your husband?* But because this wasn't her love language or what she was accustomed to, she had to start by practicing before it became natural.

Today I'm quite thankful for those notes on the calendar because hugging has become a natural way that she expresses affection toward me, but initially I had to get over the fact that she isn't naturally wired like I am. I had to accept our difference. Again, practice doesn't make perfect, it makes what you're practicing permanent.

How are you planning to demonstrate that you care?

What day this week?

- Monday
- Tuesday

- Wednesday
- Thursday
- Friday
- Saturday
- Sunday

What time?

NOTES

CHALLENGE SEVEN

LEVERAGE OR LET GO

Let the words of my mouth and the meditation of my heart
Be acceptable and pleasing in Your sight,
O Lord, my [firm, immovable] rock and my Redeemer.

PSALM 19:14 AMP

Review: Chapter 7 of *Two Equals One* (pages 79–93)

Now that you've been introduced to the Tiger and the Turtle, consider your communication style. Then, use the graph for reference.

What are your strengths? What can you leverage?

What are your weaknesses? What should you let go of?

TIGER: LEVERAGE	TIGER: LET GO	TURTLE: LEVERAGE	TURTLE: LET GO
• Safe and protective nature • Assertiveness • Emotive ability	• Need to win or be "right" • Adapt a posture of humility • Plans made without empathy for your partner	• Empathy: ability to name emotions • Desire for peace (without settling for artificial) • Care in verbalizing	• Fear of anger • Avoidance • Codependency

Take a moment to think about this: *Has your spouse been communicating something on a regular basis that may seem small to you? Have you addressed it?*

Today's challenge is to make it a priority to have a conversation about the issue. Without minimizing how your spouse feels, enter their world and try to see the issue from their viewpoint by asking clarifying questions. Mirror back what you hear them say and ask them if you got it right (more on that later). Once you understand the issue clearly, ask how you can help or what changes you can make to resolve the situation.

It might sound something like:

- "I noticed you've been cleaning a lot today, and I forgot to take my shoes off when I came home. I'm going to be better about that. Did I make you feel unseen?"
- "You seemed tense when you came home, but I never asked about your day. I'm sorry if it seemed like I didn't notice you. Is there anything you want to talk about?"
- "I noticed I left my clothes on the floor again today. I'm sorry I keep forgetting—I know you mentioned that bothers you. I will do better."

Let your spouse respond and hear them out. Resist the temptation to become defensive or to shut down when they express how they feel. The goal is to listen to understand—not simply to listen and offer a ready response or solution for their feelings.

Any assurances made in this exercise will require follow-through. Doing these things will help your spouse feel acknowledged and cared for. When we address the "small" things our spouses care about, we honor them. In his letter to the Romans, Paul tells us to "love one another with brotherly affection. Outdo one another in showing honor" (12:10). In other words, even if you don't think leaving dirty dishes in the sink is a big deal, cleaning them is an opportunity to show your spouse honor. These small behavior changes are simple, unselfish ways to communicate love. They show that you're on the same team, that your spouse's feelings are important to you, that their perspective is valid, and that you care.

Is there something your spouse has shared repeatedly that you haven't addressed? Is it a fracture that could create distance between you and your spouse? If you can't think of something, ask them if you are missing anything.

JIMMY

Let's put this in real terms. As a Tiger, sometimes the very thing I needed to let go of was the *way* in which I expressed a want or need. It wasn't that I didn't communicate, but my approach needed to factor in the Turtle I was married to. You see, the Tiger likes to control a situation, which means that my language did not often communicate or show affection, honor, or love.

Instead of hearing a request (like the ones earlier) about taking my shoes off when I came home from work as a way of showing consideration, or of showing appreciation for how hard Irene had been working that day, I would respond with something like "I pay the mortgage around here, so I should be able to wear my shoes in the house."

Usually this was coming from a defensive place—a reactive expression of the stress I was feeling. I needed to let go of my desire to lash out, the temptation to throw what I was feeling at Irene. Letting go allowed me to leverage my emotional awareness and the ability to express my wants and needs in a way that would be received.

What does this look like? For example:

Let Go: "Hey—I just got home. I don't wanna be nagged right now!"
Leverage: "Today felt like it was about everyone except me. I'm feeling really drained."

Do you hear the difference? One is all about defense, and the implication is that I'm right and you're annoying. The second is an unguarded admission—it invites the care that I'm ultimately seeking as a result of a stressful day. And unless your spouse followed you around all day (unlikely), they have no way of knowing where you're at mentally or emotionally. When we dump on them, it doesn't help them see us better and can actually make it harder for them to understand where we're coming from.

Likewise, the Turtles out there can't expect their spouse to read their minds or presume to know their spouse's motives. For example, let's say you've had a long day and really want a hug, but your spouse doesn't initiate one. It can be easy to make up a script that your spouse didn't want to hug you, that they're mad at you or simply don't love you. When in reality, if you had simply said, "I've had a rough day—I could really use a hug," you could have invited them into your need. You would have given them an opportunity to come through for you and to help.

As another example:

Let's say that what you should've expressed was a feeling of want or need. It could be physical touch, help on a task, or an affirmation. Don't stuff it.

Let go of the impulse to hide or camouflage your feelings.
Leverage the natural care you take in verbalizing.

Don't make excuses or try to tell yourself that it's not important. Even if it seems "too late" to say anything, expressing your feelings to your spouse is the only way they can truly come alongside you.

Today's challenge is simply to address a thing that seems meaningless to you but that you know is meaningful to your spouse.

Before you address this need, however, write down what you need to **let go** of and what you need to **leverage** below.

The love between you will grow in an incredible way as you honor your spouse's needs and feelings; the Tiger and the Turtle can coexist!

Let Go:

Leverage:

NOTES

CHALLENGE EIGHT

SELF CHECK-IN

Examine me, O Lord, and try me;
Test my heart and my mind.

PSALM 26:2 AMP

Review: Chapter 8 of *Two Equals One* (pages 95–109)

Traveling has become such a constant feature in our weekly life that self-check at the airport is practically routine. This constant traveling also means we've heard the safety speech more times than we can count. You know, the one where the flight attendant gives you worst-case scenarios and tells you that in the case of emergency (i.e., if you're on an airplane that's about to go down), the oxygen masks will drop. The flight attendant then advises you to put your own mask on first before helping anyone else. In the same way that we can't give oxygen to someone else if we're suffocating, we can't help our spouse navigate their emotional needs until we check ours.

Today's challenge is to do an emotional self-check. Be as honest as possible with these questions. You may be tempted to gloss over one or more touchpoints—don't. You'll never be able to fully express your needs to your spouse until you're willing to admit them to yourself. This is your oxygen mask.

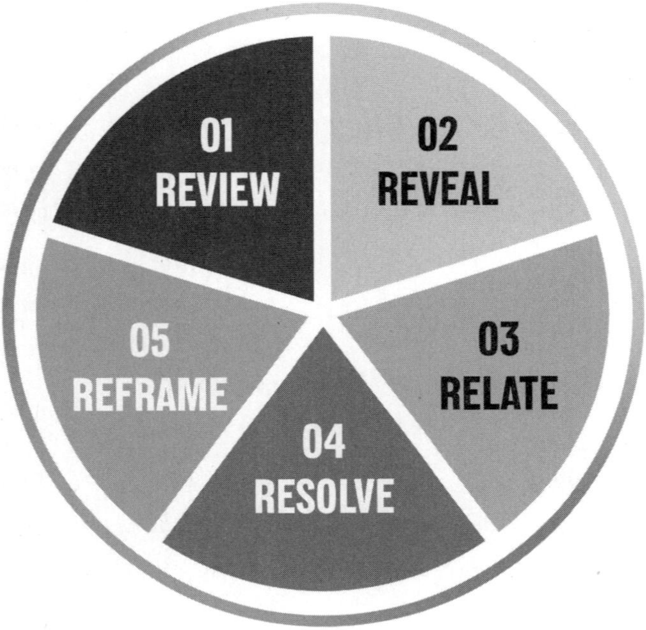

Write down an issue that has been coming up for you and your spouse. We typically categorize issues on a scale of 1–5. One is an annoyance, whereas five is something serious enough to be guided by a professional counselor. For the purpose of this exercise, use a level one issue. Then ask yourself the following questions:

1. **Review:** Determine the level one issue and write it down in the space below.

2. **Reveal:** Ask, *How does this issue make me feel?* Be descriptive.

3. **Relate:** Ask, *What could my spouse be feeling that they're not making known to me? Have I been intentional about making space for them to communicate their feelings? How could I come into their world and see it from their perspective?*

4. **Resolve:** Ask, *Is this something to say to them or something to search within me? Is this resolvable or simply manageable? Is it even worth bringing up?* Write it down in the space below and we'll talk about when to discuss it in a later challenge.

5. **Reframe:** Ask, *How could I see this differently?* Because when I see it differently, I can define it differently. Does this belong to me, or does it belong to them and is therefore their work to do? Remember: it's not personal if it belongs to them and is their work to do.

NOTES

CHALLENGE NINE

REMOTE CONTROL | CONTROLLING YOUR EMOTIONS AND NOT LETTING THEM CONTROL YOU

Your feelings are trying to tell you something: Emotional intelligence is the ability to tap in and listen to what they have to say.

***TWO EQUALS ONE*, PAGE 97**

Review: Chapter 9 of *Two Equals One* (pages 111–24)

On page 97 we talked about EQ, or emotional intelligence. Your IQ will generally remain the same, but your EQ can grow. Everyone has the potential for emotional health, but we all have to work on our EQ. Now, some may say that talking to yourself makes you look crazy. We, however, would argue that not checking in with yourself, not asking yourself these questions, can lead to *actual* crazy! Think about it: If we don't take the time to look inward and actually know what we're feeling, how can we express those feelings to our spouse? How can we expect them to navigate our emotions if we don't understand them ourselves? A lack of emotional awareness places our emotions in charge of us rather than us being in charge of our emotions.

There's an ancient proverb that says, "The purposes of a person's heart are deep waters, but one who has insight draws them out" (Proverbs 20:5 NIV). There is a reason we think how we think. There is a reason we say what we say. There is a reason we do what we do.

***TWO EQUALS ONE*, PAGE 122**

JIMMY

When I was growing up, I loved remote control cars. The problem is when the car gets too far away from the controller, you lose your ability to steer it. The car then usually veers off in the wrong direction or crashes into an obstacle. Likewise, your emotions need to stay close to you. If they get out of range, you're no longer in charge. And often our emotions lead us in the wrong direction or crash us into an argument or poor decision-making.

Checking in and asking these few simple questions is a free and painless way to untangle yourself from your emotions. Instead of allowing your emotions to pull you in all directions, you take back control.

Individually walk through steps one and two on the Seven Steps to Emotional Health. Ask yourself, *How do I feel?* Think through your emotions and then ask, *What is my behavior telling me?*

You might find that you're feeling anxious or sad. Maybe you're feeling hopeful or expectant. Whatever emotion you write down, consider what it's telling you.

Now that you both have answered questions one and two, it's time to talk through your responses. Remember that step three of the Seven Steps to Emotional Health is actually to question your opinion, and in this exercise the goal is to invite your spouse's input. We are not suggesting that you should tell your spouse what they feel (absolutely never advisable), but it can be helpful to consider each other's insights as to what your potential triggers may be.

Remember that as you discuss each other's emotional responses, your job is to help draw out the deep water that we talked about in chapter 9. Think about observed behaviors you've noted that relate to their current emotion. What is the common denominator? Try to help your spouse trace the origin of their emotion and help them grow in emotional intelligence. Use the numbers below as prompts to list emotions, related behaviors, and/or other insights that emerge from your conversation.

1.
2.
3.
4.
5.
6.
7.

CHALLENGE TEN

INTO THE DEEP

It's a risk to let someone else into the deepest places of your soul. But if you want a two-equals-one marriage, you have to learn to trust each other enough to go there.

***TWO EQUALS ONE*, PAGE 136**

Review: Chapter 10 of *Two Equals One* (pages 125–38)

The purpose of the check-in is to ensure that you don't check out. We've seen so many people check out of their marriage. They're technically still married, but they're no longer present emotionally or willing to do the work of marriage. Remember: you're not allowed to complain about a marriage you've checked out of.

We were coaching a couple once and the wife was openly sharing her feelings and emotions. As she poured her heart out, we watched the husband utterly disconnected, slouching in his chair and staring at the carpet. He seemed completely detached. He had checked out.

To our surprise, when it was his turn to talk, he went on and on . . . and on! There was a database of built-up resentment—feelings that had accumulated over the course of years. He was expressing all at once to us what he should have been communicating to her over the years. If he had simply talked out his feelings on a regular basis, if he had checked in with her regularly and communicated his needs, he would never have checked out.

One attempt at checking in with your spouse will not fix everything, but consistent check-ins can go a long way! Today's challenge is to schedule a weekly check-in. Sit down with your spouse and decide on a thirty-minute window every week where you can talk about what you're going through. If necessary or helpful, make a vulnerable request of your spouse before your check-in.

When you fly, checking a bag requires assistance from someone else. A carry-on is your responsibility, which is honestly why sometimes we don't want a carry-on! Sometimes we actually argue over whether we want the hassle, like "Why are you carrying all that?"

What we have to recognize is that we all have metaphorical baggage to check—things that require our spouse's assistance to navigate. It is our responsibility to communicate those needs. Some of our junk is carry-on—stuff that is ours to work on and not our spouse's responsibility. It's still important to communicate, but the check-in allows us to sort things out.

In the days leading up to your scheduled check-in, keep a list of things you want to discuss. When your spouse annoys you, write it down. Be specific and thoughtful in what you include, but don't let it alter your behavior toward your spouse—don't let a single instance or disagreement ruin an entire week. Things will become a lot less urgent when you stop letting your emotions control your behavior.

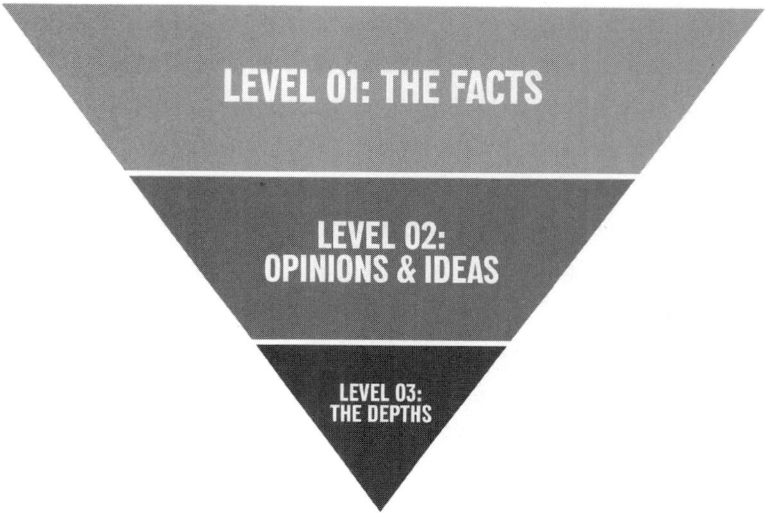

Some things you write down on Saturday won't be important come Friday. Don't let the things that annoy you dictate your behavior.

Looking at your list, choose your top three points of discussion and use the steps we've discussed.

Ask your spouse if they would like you to submit the list to them the day before your check-in. If what you're writing down is too heavy, consider whether you should bring it to a counselor.

Obviously, the goal is that you are doing some sort of check-in every day. But we've found it's also very helpful to have something on the calendar every week for the crucial conversations. During these weekly check-ins, don't hold back. Before the conversation, take a moment to gather your thoughts. Check in with yourself, and be really honest about how you are feeling. Then go into the conversation determined to share those feelings authentically with your spouse while using these tools to see if you can draw the deep water from them.

What's really going on in your spouse's heart? As Proverbs reminds us, there is deep water down there; your job is to use any insight you have to draw it out. You are trying to dive beneath the facts, the assumptions, and your ideas about how they should be doing and get down to what is really going on.

***TWO EQUALS ONE*, PAGE 133**

Every week doesn't have to look the same. Mix it up and have some fun with it! Go to different places, talk about different things, and even when the topics of conversation end up being heavy, find a way to keep the experience uplifting by always choosing to love each other. Be intentional by filling out the line below:

Scheduled date of check-in: ____________ Time: ____________

The five Rs—Review, Reveal, Relate, Resolve, Reframe—can be helpful when processing issues that come up. For example, if your spouse says or does something that hurts your feelings, ask yourself:

1. What bothered me about that?
2. How does this issue make me feel? Be descriptive.
3. What could my spouse be feeling that they're not making known to me? How could I come into their world and see it from their perspective?
4. Is this something to say to them or something to search within me? Is this resolvable or simply manageable? Is it even worth

bringing up? Write it down in the blank space below, and we'll talk about when to discuss it in a later challenge.

5. "Does this belong to me, or does it belong to them and is therefore their work to do?" Remember: it's not personal if it belongs to them and is their work to do.

The next day, review your notes. So, let's say the infraction happened on a Tuesday; check in with yourself on Wednesday and ask, *"Is this still bothering me? Is this my work or theirs? Is this making the list?"*

After your check-in, ask yourself, *How did it go?* Keep a record so that you can observe improvement!

NOTES

CHALLENGE ELEVEN

TWO TRUTHS AND A LIE

When we're doing coaching sessions with other couples, you can always tell which couple has some conflict between them, because they are hesitant to do any of the exercises with each other. That usually means that something happened and they haven't addressed it. As if there's an elephant in the room, but they've managed to put a curtain around it and ignore it. Checking in forces you to pull back the curtain.

***TWO EQUALS ONE*, PAGE 141**

Review: Chapter 11 of *Two Equals One* (pages 139–48)

For this challenge, let's play Two Truths and a Lie . . . a modified version.

Take some time to sit down with your spouse and identify one or more lies that you have been believing. They may be old wounds, they may be self-doubt, they may mostly surface in the form of insecurities or anxiety. List ways you doubt yourself or fears that creep up on you.

Write them down.

Now, replace them with two truths. The first truth will be a scripture that refutes the lie, but the second truth will take the lie, that false thought, and turn it around in order to create an affirmation for yourself.

It will look something like this:

Lie: I am not enough.
God's Truth: "For we are God's masterpiece. He has created us anew in Christ Jesus, so we can do the good things he planned for us long ago." (Ephesians 2:10 NLT)
My Truth: God uniquely created me with purpose. He says I am enough.

Lie: I am afraid I'm going to fail.
God's Truth: "For I can do everything through Christ, who gives me strength." (Philippians 4:13 NLT)
My Truth: I don't rely on my strength, but God's. I am more than capable.

Take some time to review each other's lies together. Take turns affirming each other and speaking truth over one another. Confront the lies. Those lies are holding you back, so speaking truth over each other is claiming victory for both of you!

JIMMY

If you've been paying attention, at this point you are fully aware that I am the outwardly affectionate one in our relationship. This at times has actually been a source of insecurity and frustration. I created false narratives in my head about why she rarely initiated or so rarely showed physical affection. I would tell myself, *Irene doesn't love me.*

Growing up in church I was fully aware of the Ten Commandments. I knew that in Exodus 20:16 it says not to "bear false witness" (NKJV). What I didn't realize was what exactly that meant; it means that you should never decide or declare something untrue about someone else. The reason God tells us this is because we can't see or know the motives of a person's heart. I didn't understand that Irene felt unloved growing up and hadn't been shown affection the way I had. She didn't have a healthy gauge for that kind of interaction. I also had to recognize that just because I initiate it, the affection she gives back is no less sincere or valid.

Lie: Irene doesn't love me.

God's Truth: "You shall not bear false witness against your neighbor." (Exodus 20:16 NKJV)

My Truth: Irene loves me. Physical touch is my natural response, and it's okay for me to initiate affection. Irene expresses love in many other ways that are no less genuine.

Now, enter one or more of your own two truths and a lie in the space below:

Lie:

God's Truth:

My Truth:

NOTES

CHALLENGE TWELVE

FEARS AREN'T FINAL

This isn't about ditching everything from before you were married, but your spouse should take priority. This is true for each of you; if one of you has an issue, you both have an issue.

***TWO EQUALS ONE*, PAGE 153**

Review: Chapter 12 of *Two Equals One* (pages 153–65)

One couple we coached had been married only a few months and were already feeling a strain on their relationship. Unanswered questions, unspoken requests, and unmet expectations were all converging. Fear had entered the chat. Fear was telling this couple that the change of simply becoming husband and wife had somehow invalidated their love—that the excitement and thrill were gone forever.

In seasons of transition, it can become all the more challenging to prioritize time together. Whether due to busyness or the foreignness of change, seasons can make us feel distant from our spouse—as though we've grown apart.

What was the latest transition you experienced in your marriage? Are you newlyweds, transitioning from singlehood to married life? If you're new parents, maybe you're awkwardly making the transition into becoming a mother or father. Maybe it's a new job or the loss of a parent. Whatever it is, write it down. Here are a few examples to get you started:

Write four fears that you're experiencing as a result of this transition. Where do they come from? In the example provided, we reference memories because typically our fear of the future has roots in our past.

Identify the fears and write them down. Ask yourself, *Where do they come from?* Then ask yourself, *How can my spouse help me address these fears?*

Maybe it's a fear of abandonment or a fear of betrayal. Maybe you're afraid of failing or a financial burden is weighing you down. Maybe the reason it's been bothering you is simply that you don't think your spouse will care about it. But no matter how trivial the fear may seem, write it down. Then, using the diagram above, connect memories to each expressed fear. When you're done, it will look something like the example provided earlier.

Now discuss your diagram with your spouse. Talk about each associated memory. Don't rush this. Discuss ways that you can relate to each other's feelings and ways you can help encourage each other moving forward.

Change is inevitable, but we don't have to—and as a married couple, shouldn't—go through it alone. Fear often masquerades as an expected outcome based on past experiences, heightened anxieties, or untruths. Fear is what you make up about something before it ever happens. When we come together, we remove the mask and uncover the truth.

Fight the feeling that fears are final.

When you face the fear, your remove the facade. You fix your eyes on the greater future.

Remember that your spouse is your safe place. The Enemy wants you to believe that your hurt is forever, but change can be healing when we walk out real love in times that would otherwise simply be hard. When you remove the mask, you can actually rest in the comfort of being fully known, of being seen and heard. That is true intimacy.

Four Fears:

1.
2.
3.
4.

NOTES

CHALLENGE THIRTEEN

MAPPING BACKWARD TO MOVE FORWARD

The thing about your past is that it has the capacity to enrich your future. It can become your testimony; it can deepen your intimacy, and instead of being a stronghold pulling you backward, it can strengthen your relationship and propel you forward. But you have to face it. Stop and think about that. Are you willing to confront your past so that you and your spouse can have the future God wants for you? To have the future he designed for you?

***TWO EQUALS ONE*, PAGE 170**

Review: Chapter 13 of *Two Equals One* (pages 167–80)

Does the idea of "extreme ownership" that we talked about in chapter 13 make you uncomfortable? In all honesty, sometimes it is uncomfortable. But it's necessary for all of us in order to become emotionally healthy. It's necessary in order to connect on any kind of meaningful level with your spouse.

We talked about mapping your triggers, but since *mapping* is a term that has been misused, we want to be very clear: This is a deeply introspective tool. The reason we advise that the initial steps be done independently is that the emotions you are feeling are connected to your personal, individual memories. Up until this point you've been practicing naming your emotions, but this is a step deeper.

Today's challenge is to map that emotion. This may make you uncomfortable, but working independently, ask yourself (do not say anything out loud yet), *When was the last time the two of us were in an argument?* Or if you've been avoiding an argument for some time, *When was the last time my spouse annoyed me?*

Before either of you says anything audibly, take some time to trace that emotion backward. Moving ahead requires mapping backward. Remember, this isn't about rehashing what you were arguing about or determining any blame. This is about tracing the origin of your emotion and understanding your trigger. We are not trying to prove anything in this exercise—we're looking to understand.

Ask yourself: *Why did I feel that way? Was it anger, shame, fear, or grief?*

Use the lines provided and follow the five Cs in the stair-step diagram. Go backward as far as you can. You will know when you've arrived at the source because there will be mental clarity instead of simply emotion.

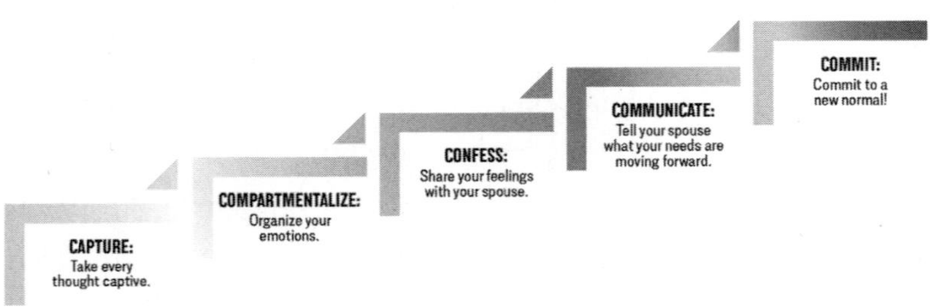

- **Capture:** Name the emotion.
- **Compartmentalize:** Trace the origin. This is yours—your spouse cannot do this for you. Own the work that is yours to do.
- **Confess:** Be honest with yourself about how you felt and where the emotion started. Even though this may be a traumatic memory, embrace that it happened: Do not avoid it. This didn't just happen *to* you, it happened *for* you. When you take ownership of your emotions, you gain back power.
- **Communicate:** Write a list of what you need or want to be on the healthy side of your emotions. Write what you want to tell your spouse about this emotion.
- **Commit:** Commit to a new normal and list specific things you agree to do for each other moving forward. Make this list attainable. It's important that you agree that this is something you can and are willing to try.

At this point, you and your spouse can take turns sharing your maps. If it helps, have a baton or some object you can pass back and forth to visually represent whose turn it is to talk. Resist the urge to interrupt one another—it's very important you let each other finish talking. You both want and need to be heard.

As you do this, be as honest and vulnerable as possible. Again, this isn't about being right; it's about being understood. It is important for the health of your relationship that you are both able to share the process. When did you feel triggered? What was the emotion? Ask yourself, *What's coming up for me?* Then walk your spouse back to the origin and express what you need moving forward.

Take ownership.

Avoid accusatory language and focus on your responsibility in the situation.

Then, make your commitments to one another.

Be specific and realistic.

If it was a phrase or word that triggered your spouse, it's realistic to say that you won't use that language in your home in the future. It's not realistic to ask your spouse to never speak to your mother-in-law again! Make sure that what you commit to is attainable and helpful because follow-through builds trust, whereas a lack of fulfillment is destructive.

Capture:

Compartmentalize:

Confess:

Communicate:

Commit:

CHALLENGE FOURTEEN

MARRIAGE CONTINUUM

A person standing alone can be attacked and defeated, but two can stand back-to-back and conquer. Three are even better, for a triple-braided cord is not easily broken.

ECCLESIASTES 4:12 NLT

Review: Chapter 14 of *Two Equals One* (pages 181–89)

The marriage continuum is something we get so excited about! It's a tool to establish vision with one another for the future, even while encouraging each other along the way. It's a way to reinforce that you are both on the same team—to show that when you work together, you win together.

Today's challenge is to openly share a time when your spouse helped you move through the marriage continuum.

- Maybe you were stuck in hurting when your spouse found resources for you both to improve your relationship.
- Maybe a moment where your spouse displayed a willingness to do the work and gave you hope.
- Even the simple act of reading *Two Equals One* and this workbook together is an effort to build your relationship and should not be overlooked.

Whatever the instance, be specific and take the time to express your appreciation. This is an opportunity to move forward in the marriage continuum as you encourage one another on the journey. Celebrate and champion each other's initiatives. Make sure your spouse knows that you see them and their efforts and that they have positively impacted you. Remember: you are on the same team!

CHALLENGE FIFTEEN

WEAKNESSES BECOMING STRENGTHS

It's not about mine versus yours—it's about us as one. When we look at two equals one this way, we're able to appreciate each other's strengths and not feel jealous when the other's strengths are in the spotlight.

***TWO EQUALS ONE*, PAGE 185**

Review: Chapter 15 of *Two Equals One* (pages 191–200)

As you were reading chapter 15, what came to mind? Did you think about attributes or traits of your spouse? Did you compare your gifts to theirs?

Take some time to celebrate the intrinsic gifts you've observed in your spouse. There is a list of personality assessments in the back of *Two Equals One*, and if you haven't already, we highly recommend taking them, but for the purpose of this exercise, your observations will suffice.

Today's challenge will take more or less time depending on your willingness. We want to encourage you that if you're truly honest on this exercise, it will become an invaluable tool moving forward. A tool of insight and communication. This is an opportunity to talk about your spouse's qualities, their natural talents. To note specific instances where their gifts have positively affected you.

The more specific, the better. Don't be defensive if their strength is also your weakness—this is part of the equation. Remember: Their strength is a gift that you married! It's meant to complement you, not compete.

PART 1: YOUR SPOUSE'S STRENGTHS

Either grab a notebook or pull out your phone and start a new list. Write your spouse's name and then the word *strengths*. Spend the next three minutes writing out three of your spouse's strengths.

1.

2.

3.

Now, look at your spouse and take turns telling each other about your list. Don't rush this process—it can be tempting to just name each one, but be descriptive. It can be helpful to add the phrase "for example." You might say, "You are great at raising the kids. For example, last week I noticed you . . ."

This may feel awkward at first, but it's a great exercise to keep doing on a regular basis. Recognizing your spouse's strengths and actually saying them out loud is not something we naturally do day in and day out, but it is essential for navigating differences. Don't be discouraged if it feels strained at first. Think of it like a muscle—like going to the gym. It's challenging at first, but with practice, it gets easier, and you reap a benefit that is actually visible!

PART 2: YOUR OWN WEAKNESSES

If you thought talking about strengths was awkward, you're probably cringing at the thought of talking about weaknesses! But hang in there with us. This exercise requires some humility and the understanding that your spouse's weaknesses are an opportunity to know, love, and appreciate them more. Don't feel like you have to be perfect—we all have weaknesses, and a huge part of this marriage equation is embracing each other's weaknesses.

For this part, create a new category, but this time it's for yourself. Instead of pointing out your spouse's weaknesses, make a list of three of your own shortcomings:

1.
2.
3.

Now, share your list with your spouse, owning your weaknesses and not trying to explain them or make excuses. Although we won't press into examples this round, this exercise can be a great opportunity to own up to things with your spouse. For instance: "One of my weaknesses is staying present and really listening when you talk. Last night when you were talking about your day, I was distracted by work, and I could've done a better job being in that conversation with you."

Once you talk through your strengths and weaknesses, pay attention to how you feel. Chances are you feel closer than you have in a long time.

PART 3: OBSERVED BEHAVIOR

The next part of this challenge may require some time to process. Don't rush it. This is where you each identify a potentially learned behavior you've observed in your spouse. This is not about making an accusation—all you're doing is observing a behavior and telling your spouse how it makes you feel.

Note: what may seem odd to you may actually reflect more about your own upbringing than theirs.

Some friends of ours once did this exercise. The wife wrote that when her husband encouraged them to fast (the Christian practice of abstaining from specific foods in order to prioritize God), she felt pressured and self-conscious about her weight. What she couldn't see prior to talking through her feelings was that her previous battles with an eating disorder had clouded her perspective on fasting. What he saw as purely spiritual easily became connected to diet for her. While he was resisting some of his favorite foods and thereby clearing his heart and mind, she was resisting the foods but simultaneously counting calories. Diet was a trigger that had in the past prompted her into a downhill spiral. After their conversation, they were able to navigate fasting together by avoiding fasts that were strictly food-based.

What you write may end up actually telling you something about yourself that you didn't see before. Approach what you observe with humility and be sure to give your spouse time to process. It's possible that your spouse has never considered their behavior "abnormal."

Be sure to own your own emotion.

Individually fill in the blanks of this sentence:

"When I see you do or say __________, I feel ________."

After you read each other's sentence, take a moment to reflect on the behavior that your spouse has observed. Try to find a way to relate to your spouse's emotion. Avoid becoming defensive—remember that your spouse is *for* you. Listen and consider what motivates your behavior. Then consider where you may have learned this behavior.

Is the behavior intrinsic or is it something you can unlearn?

These conversations are part of drawing a blueprint—they build into hard conversations that are necessary when navigating transitions. Ever watched a home be constructed? Before the builders can even lay the foundation, there needs to be a blueprint—a map charting the way. These conversations are putting ink on the paper so that you can build toward longevity, so that you can create something lasting.

Now you will be able to benefit from your spouse's strengths! When you feel weak, you can embrace the ways they complement you.

NOTES

CHALLENGE SIXTEEN

RECLAIM TERRITORY

"Take off your sandals from your feet, for the place where you are standing is holy."

JOSHUA 5:15

Review: Chapter 16 of *Two Equals One* (pages 201–10)

Do you have ugly mile markers like we talked about in chapter 16? Places that remind you of painful moments? Maybe it's a room where you had a particularly bad fight or a fist-shaped hole in the wall that left an emotional scar. Whatever it is, it's time to reclaim some territory.

In Joshua 5:15 the Lord meets with Joshua face-to-face before the Israelites take the promised land. He says to him, "Take off your sandals from your feet, for the place where you are standing is holy." These were the same words spoken to Moses, Joshua's predecessor—once again, as he stood in the Lord's presence.

If we want the same anointing of presence, we, too, need to be intentional of our space. This is more than just going barefoot. It's about making reparations for past hurts.

As a starting point, make a list together of places, starting in your home, that evoke a painful memory in your relationship. Be honest and vulnerable with each other as you make this list. This is not about settling old scores—it's about coming together and reclaiming your marriage. Next,

- Go around to each place you listed and pray together over each.
- Be specific.
- Denounce any lies or hurtful words thrown in the heat of an argument.
- Replace each with a truth and an affirmation.

Don't rush through this. This is your opportunity to honor one another and show the impassioned love that God commands us to have for each other.

CHALLENGE SEVENTEEN

COUPLE BUBBLE

What Jimmy and I have learned (albeit the hard way) is that God wants to turn your traumas and tragedies into trophies. He wants to give you victory.

***TWO EQUALS ONE*, PAGE 204**

Review: Chapter 17 of *Two Equals One* (pages 211–19)

Another couple we coached struggled in the beginning of their marriage to set boundaries with friends and family. They both felt guilty for saying no to invitations, or they felt as though they were missing out.

Years down the road and in a much healthier place, we were talking with this same couple about friend groups. Because they had taken the "couple bubble" (diagram on the next page) to heart and applied it, they could look back and clearly see how they had influenced the friends around them. By prioritizing their marriage, they had inspired growth—and not just in their own marriage. Those around them began to work on creating healthy boundaries and investing in their spouses too!

Let's be clear: Boundaries aren't about limiting your life or treating you like a child. As we said in chapter 17, this is about ownership. This is about making deliberate choices in our lives that will ensure we have the future we want.

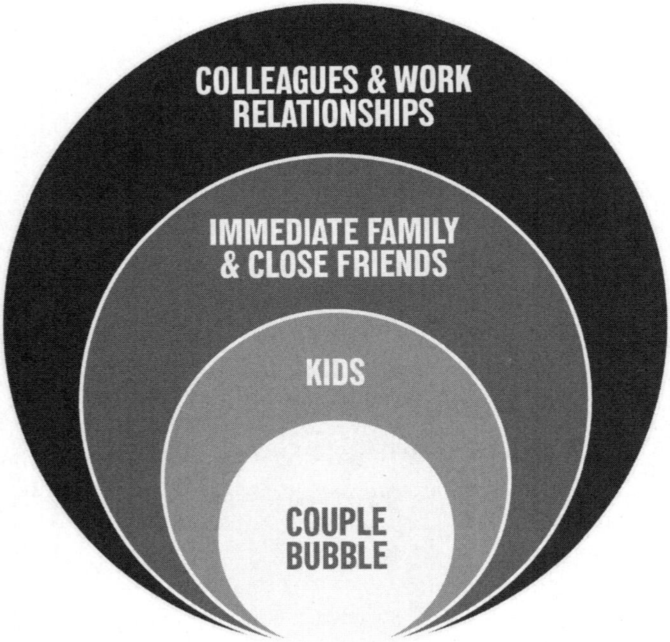

Take some time today to talk with your spouse about areas in your life that need boundaries.

Individually, write out areas that are a source of stumbling for you. It doesn't have to be a sin issue; it can simply be things that cause you frustration or that could potentially invade your safe place. It could be relationships you find draining, tasks where you would like to share responsibility, or something related to your budget. Take turns talking through your list.

As you do, consider creating a "signal word" or phrase that is known only between the two of you. Something to use when you're out in public and feel your safe place or "couple bubble" is being encroached.

Remember that boundaries protect—they exist not to limit you, but to ensure that you and your spouse operate as a team, that you champion each other's strengths and guard each other's weaknesses.

If it concerns your spouse, it should concern you too.

***TWO EQUALS ONE*, PAGE 215**

If you feel stuck and aren't sure what areas apply to your marriage, ask each other questions like "What can I do to make you feel safe when I deal with coworkers of the opposite sex?" or "We love our kids, but one day it'll just be the two of us again. Let's start practicing now."

Now make a plan to put boundaries in place. Write ways that you can support one another and ensure that you are both cared for.

NOTES

CHALLENGE EIGHTEEN

PUT A RING ON IT

Review: Chapter 18 of *Two Equals One* (pages 221–29)

There's one last challenge we want to offer you . . . It's something we do at every Two Equals One conference and retreat.

For this challenge, you will need a Ring Pop. Yes, we mean the oversized candy ring that you used to covet as a kid!

Now, take a deep breath (grab a breath mint first!) and, looking your spouse in the eyes, repeat these vows:

> I vow not to allow differences to divide us but to complete us.
>
> I vow to make our marriage my first priority.
>
> I vow to forgive fast and focus on the future.
>
> I vow to live beyond myself, love beyond my preferences, and laugh beyond my struggles.
>
> I vow to work on my relationship with God, so that expressing my love for you comes from an overflow of that.
>
> I vow to have a love that has the capacity to hold your humanity.
>
> With this ring, I will savor the sweetness of our marriage.
>
> I will love you always and forever.

Finally, slip the Ring Pop on his or her finger, and you may kiss your spouse!

ADDITIONAL RESOURCES

Jimmy and I are here to help! This is what we do. We offer individualized coaching, couples Soulscapes, and marriage seminars. www.twoequalsone.com

Suicide Help

- Suicide Hotline: 1-800-273-8255

Domestic Violence Help

- National Domestic Violence Helpline: 1-800-799-7233

Substance Abuse and Mental Health Recovery

- Al-Anon: www.al-anon.org
- Celebrate Recovery: www.celebraterecovery.com
- Certified Sex Addiction Therapist: www.iitap.com
- Co-Dependents Anonymous: www.coda.org
- Covenant Eyes: www.covenanteyes.com
- Gentle Path: www.themeadows.com/about/locations/gentlepath/

- Rio Retreat Center: https://rioretreatcenter.com/
- Honey Lake Clinic: www.honeylake.clinic
- Life Healing Center: www.sierratucson.com
- Recovery Ranch: www.recoveryranch.com/mental-health-treatment-programs-nashville-tn/process-addiction-treatment-center/sex-addiction-treatment-center
- Sex Addiction Intensives: www.drdougweiss.com/intensives/addiction-intensive
- Substance Abuse and Mental Health Services Administration: www.samhsa.gov

Personality Profiles

- DiSC Profile: http://discprofile.com
- Enneagram Personality Test: www.enneagramtest.com
- Love Language Quiz: http://5lovelanguages.com

Counseling/Coaching

- A Place of HOPE Counseling Center: http://www.aplaceofhope.com
- Crossroads Counseling of the Rockies: www.crossroadscounseling.net
- Heart to Heart Counseling: www.drdougweiss.com/addiction-intensive
- Imago Relationship Therapists: www.imagorelationshipswork.com
- Onsite: https://experienceonsite.com
- Marriage 180 Intensive: https://relationship180.com/intensives/#
- The Meadows Treatment Center: www.themeadows.com

NOTE TO THE READER

We get many opportunities to be a part of weddings, but often couples focus so much on the wedding, little thought or work is given to the marriage. Thank you for taking the time to read this book and to do the work of marriage!

ABOUT THE AUTHORS

Jimmy and Irene Rollins are passionate about ministry, but even more so they are passionate about marriage and the family unit. *Two Equals One is all about bringing these two passions together!* The mission is simple: build healthy marriages that result in healthy families, having an impact on our communities for the better.

After almost twenty-five years of full-time ministry, ten of which they served as senior pastors of i5 City, a thriving church with over three thousand members, Jimmy and Irene felt a shift in their ministry focus. They transitioned from their roles as senior pastors and yielded to the call on their lives—a call to help others build healthy marriages and families filled with *love*, *laughter*, and *longevity*.

Throughout their own marriage, Jimmy and Irene have navigated many difficulties in their relationship, including food and alcohol addictions, family dysfunction, and communication issues as well as many painful seasons of loss. For the first fifteen years of marriage, Jimmy and Irene were, as they say, "surviving but not thriving." They did their best to manage the many challenges of family life while simultaneously navigating the complexities and nuances of their professional and ministry life.

It all came to a screeching halt in 2015 when the demands of their public professional ministry life and private family and marriage life became too much for two broken individuals to manage. It was time to get help and pursue the healing they desperately needed.

Now living their best life, Jimmy and Irene are sought after globally as dynamic public speakers, authors, and marriage coaches. Offering marriage intensives for both church and corporate settings as well as individualized coaching and marriage retreats, Two Equals One is all about sharing from their wealth of experience and wisdom to inspire individuals and couples with a unique message of hope, healing, and restoration.

Jimmy is a nationally recognized speaker, marriage coach, and author who inspires diverse audiences to live beyond themselves on the journey to discovering their greater purpose. As a key strategic partner for several influential churches and parachurch organizations, Jimmy's ministry experience has been critical to architecting strategies to increase influence and realize greater impact.

Irene is a certified emotional intelligence coach and recovery activist. As a marriage educator, she loves to study human behavior and guide people to be the best version of themselves through her teaching, writing, and coaching. Irene's passion to help others overcome their self-defeating habits comes from her life experience as an overcomer of alcohol addiction and trauma.

In their downtime Jimmy and Irene enjoy reading, golfing, exercising, cooking, and clowning around with their adult children, Kayla, Jaden, and Maya, and their two English bulldog babies.